ndehaus v. Westen.

OLYMPIA / PRAGUE

ČERVENÁ

The GHETTO of Prague

The GHETTO of Prague

PHOTOS BY JIŘÍ MACHT
TEXT BY
VLADIMÍR SADEK AND JIŘINA ŠEDINOVÁ

OLYMPIA / PRAGUE

Interior of the Old-New Synagogue
<

The present appearance of the Old-New Synagogue and the Jewish Townhall
<<

18th century tombstones in the Old Jewish Cemetery
<<<

Western gable of the Old-New Synagogue
<<<<

The Old-New Synagogue from Maisel Street
>

ISBN 80-7033-166-6

Vestibule of the Old-New Synagogue
was built in the Romanesque style. There is
a pulpit for the Cantor's prayer book, the
benches and treasury boxes from the
17th century for the Jewish tax

The tympanum of the entrance to the Old-New Synagogue
is decorated with the motif of vine and grapes the number of which symbolizes the twelve tribes of Israel

The windows in the women's aisle in the Old-New Synagogue
The main hall of the Synagogue was initially used by men only. The women's aisle was added at a later date, and the women followed the service through its narrow windows

Chair of the Chief Rabbi in the Old-New Synagogue
is situated in the place where the famous Rabbi Jehuda Liwa ben Bezalel, known as Rabbi Löw, used to sit during his lifetime

the women could follow the ceremony through narrow windows. The interior decoration of the Old-New Synagogue is severe, but deeply impressive. Apart from architectural decorative elements it consists of Hebrew wall inscriptions quoting in an abbreviated form some biblical verses or talmudic quotations. The centre of the hall is occupied by the lectern ("bima", "almemor") surrounded with a richly moulded grate. That is the place of wedding ceremonies and of the reading of the Hebrew texts of the Pentateuch, the Torah (i.e. Law) forming the spiritual basis of Jewish religion and one of the foundation stones of European culture in general. When not used for reading the Torah scrolls are deposited in the Ark ("aron ha-kodesh") situated at the eastern wall of the synagogue, in the direction of Jerusalem towards which all prayers of the believers were oriented. In front of the Ark there is the cantor's place and also a stone bench on which the circumcision ceremony had been performed in the past. Somewhat to the side there is the chair of the Chief Rabbi in which the famous Rabbi Löw used to sit according to tradition. In the Old-New Synagogue also the historical banner of the Prague Jewish Community has been preserved, decorated with David's star and the Jewish hat.

The second oldest monument of the Prague ghetto is the Old Jewish Cemetery which had served as burying ground from the first half of the 15th century to 1787. In that year, in the framework of reforms of Emperor Joseph II, the burials were stopped for hygienic reasons and the initially plague cemetery in the present-day Fibich Street in Prague-Žižkov became the principal burial ground of Prague Jews.

At present the Old Jewish Cemetery forms an oasis of peace and contemplation in the centre of the busy city. The first feature which attracts the visitors' attention is the dense cumulation of tombstones, typical chiefly of the central part of the cemetery. With this feature the cemetery had become a symbolic representation of the Prague ghetto which always has to struggle with the shortage of space and was extremely overcrowded particularly in the 18th century. There was not enough room for the living, and there was not enough room for the dead whose graves are inviolable according to the humanist principles of Jewish religion. Therefore, in the end, it was necessary to spread new soil on top of older graves and make the burials in this new soil, while the old graves remained untouched. In this way a number of superimposed layers of graves originated in the central area of the cemetery, the tombstones of which had been always lifted to the ground surface. When some parts of the cemetery were abolished in 1903, their tombstones were moved to the preserved areas or sunk into the cemetery walls. At present a systematic restoration and conservation of the cemetery has been going on for a number of years to protect it against deteriorating ecological conditions and preserve it for future generations as a monument the religious meaning of which is combined with historical, cultural and artistic meanings. The Hebrew tombstone inscriptions namely form an important source of historical information and the decorations of many tombstones testify to the development of fine arts in the Prague ghetto. While the oldest, mediaeval tombstones are plain, various relief decorations begin to appear in the course of the Renaissance period and become particularly numerous in the subsequent Baroque. The visitor's eye can observe a diverse procession of tombstone reliefs symbolizing the origin, name or profession of the deceased. It can see the blessing hands of priests-cohens, levite's lavers, the lions, wolves, bears, deers, fishes, birds and flowers, similarly as the doctor's lancets, pharmacist's mortars, prayer books. There are also general symbols, derived from biblical and post-biblical tradition, and even human figures, decorating particularly the graves of prematurely deceased girls and young women. A walk through the cemetery acquaints the visitor simultaneously with the personalities and works of foremost Jewish scholars who had lived in Prague and found the place of their last rest in the Old Jewish Cemetery. Let us mention at least a few: Avigdor Kara (d. 1439), Jehuda Liwa ben Bezalel — Rabbi Löw (1512—1609), David Gans (1541—1613), Joseph Solomon Delmedigo (1591—1655), Issachar Bär Teller (d. 1687), Jehuda Löw Teller (d. 1697), David Oppenheim (1664—1736).

The spiritual and artistic life of the Prague ghetto was marked by the arrival and the development of the ideas of the Renaissance in the 16th and at the beginning of the 17th centuries, which fundamentally changed its way of life. The first impact of the Renaissance spirit was brought about by Hebrew book printing whose centre north of the Alps was Prague. At the beginning of the 16th century the Gersonide family printing shop originated in Prague which issued books with rich decorations, including inter alia also human figures not used until then in the Jewish communities of Central Europe for religious reasons. The development of Prague Hebrew book printing influenced also other fields of Jewish art. Under the influence of book illustrations, particularly the title pages, there originated both the decorative architectural designs of tombstones and, in some cases, the decorations of the silver Torah shields or synagogue curtains, valances and Torah mantles. The development of local Jewish book printing resulted also in the gradual widening of the intellectual horizon of the population of the Prague ghetto in spite of the deep crisis the ghetto had undergone in the middle of the 16th century in connection with the attempts to expel Jews from Prague.

In the first half of the 16th century the leading family of the Prague ghetto were the Horowitz. The number of the monuments recalling their activities in the administration and the spiritual life of the ghetto includes the Pinkas Synagogue built in 1535 by Aron Meshullam Horowitz. The deep hollow in which the synagogue is situated has been the cause of permanent trouble with ground water, moisture elevation and floods. At the break of the 16th and the 17th centuries the building was adapted by Judah Goldschmied de Herz. His work completed the still captivating charm of the building the architecture of which combines Late Gothic style with more playful Renaissance elements. After the Second World War the Pinkas Synagogue has become the deeply moving Memorial of Jewish Victims of Nazi Persecution in Bohemia and Moravia, whose names were written on the synagogue walls together with the dates of their birth, transport to concentration camp and the name of the respective Jewish community. In the course of the following years it was discovered that the moisture elevation in the synagogue walls proceeded more than it had been assumed initially. Therefore, the Pinkas Synagogue was closed for many years and underwent gradual reconstruction and installation of an insulating system. These improvements were terminated only in 1990, when it was also possible to begin with the renovation of the names of the Jewish victims of Nazism on the synagogue walls.

While the Horowitz family heralded Jewish Renaissance in the Prague ghetto, the period of Rudolphinian Renaissance was connected with the person of Mordecai Maisel. This financier of Rudolph II and Mayor of the Jewish Town of Prague made his mark in local history by an extensive reconstruction of the ghetto which he financed. He died in 1601 and his sumptuous tombstone in the Old Jewish Cemetery is situated near the tombstone of Rabbi Löw, the principal representative of the spiritual life in the Prague ghetto of the Renaissance.

Jehuda Liwa ben Bezalel — Rabbi Löw (1512—1609) — ranks among the supreme personalities of Jewish religious and philosophical thinking on the world scale. He was the head of the high talmudist school — the yeshiva — which had been founded by Mordecai Maisel together with the Klausen Synagogue, rebuilt in Baroque style after the fire in 1689. Apart from that Rabbi Löw was concerned with community matters, having elaborated inter alia also the rules of the Prague Burial Society ("Hevra kadisha"), founded in 1564. The spiritual heritage of Rabbi Löw has been preserved in a number of his writings published mostly by the Gersonide printing shop. They cover his religious philosophy, his ethics and his pedagogical ideas which are analogous with the ideas of J. A. Comenius in the Christian sphere. At the same time he anticipated in many respects the East European Hasidism of the 18th and the 19th centuries, known to modern reader from the writings of the Jewish thinker, Martin Buber, as a rule. However, Rabbi Löw is best known to the wider cultural public thanks to the legends, inspired mostly by his wisdom and venerable age. One of these legends is illustrated by the sculptural group by Ladislav Šaloun (1870—1946). The sculptures, made in the Art Nouveau (Jugendstil) represents the sage and a young girl, his grand-daughter, handing him a rose. It was inspired by the legend about the wisdom and saintliness of Rabbi Löw which were so great that even the Angel of Death could not overcome them. Finally, he concealed himself in the beautiful rose, and only after the old man had sniffed it could the Angel of Death overcome him. The most widely and best known is the legend of Golem — an artificial human being, made of clay and enlivened by the Rabbi by means of the secret name of the God ("shem").

In the Renaissance also mathematical and natural sciences were studied in the Prague ghetto. They were cultivated primarily by David Gans, historian, mathematician and astronomer, Joseph Solomon Delmedigo, physician, mathematician, astronomer and philosopher, and Issachar Bär Teller and Jehuda Löw Teller, physicians.

At the time of Mordecai Maisel, Rabbi Löw and the 17th century scholars the High Synagogue, the Maisel Synagogue, the Klausen Synagogue and the Jewish Townhall originated in the ghetto together with other buildings which did not survive the demolitions at the break of the 19th and the 20th centuries. David Gans writes in his chronicle "Zemach David" ("David's Sprig") that Mordecai Maisel "at his own expense built the High Synagogue, the resplendent sanctuary, to our glory and embellishment; he built a water reservoir for the community and a ritual bath; he built an alms-house for the poor and suffering; he had all the streets in the Jewish town paved with stone —all that with his own money and at his own cost. He also built a great synagogue, so excellent and ornate that it had none equal in beauty in the whole Diaspora . . ."

From those which have survived only the High Synagogue, founded in 1568 by Mordecai Maisel and built by the Italian master builder, Pancratius Roder, has retained its initial appearance. All other buildings were heavily damaged by fires in the 17th and the 18th centuries and subsequently rebuilt in different styles.

The High Synagogue obtained its name because its main hall is situated on the first floor of the building adjoining the Jewish Townhall. It has a pure Renaissance vault decorated with lunettes, ornamental ribs and bead mouldings. As late as before the Second World War the synagogue was used for services. After the war it became a part of the Prague Jewish Museum; at present it houses a permanent exhibition of synagogal textiles, the oldest of which, dating from the end of the 16th century, are of Prague origin.

The main hall of the High Synagogue was originally entered directly from the Jewish Townhall, once again built by Pancratius Roder on the commission of Mordecai Maisel. The Renaissance townhall fell victim to the great fire in 1689. Its final Rococo appearance was determined by the reconstruction of 1763 due to the no less devastating fire of 1754. It is from that period that the well-known Hebrew clock on the townhall turret dates, the hands of which rotate from right to left in accordance with the direction of reading and writing of Hebrew script.

The number of buildings erected by Mordecai Maisel in the Prague ghetto includes also the synagogue bearing his name until the present day. It was

completed in 1592 by the builders Joseph Wahl and Judah Goldschmied de Herz. Similarly as the other buildings also the Maisel Synagogue was heavily damaged by the fire of 1689, after which it was repaired and finally fundamentally reconstructed in the Neo-Gothic style at the break of the 19th and the 20th centuries. At present it houses the Jewish Museum exhibitions of synagogue art, the monuments of which originated in various Jewish communities in Bohemia and Moravia, liquidated during Nazi persecution in the Second World War. The majority of these monuments, many of which rank among top-level examples of silversmith's art, is related to the parchment Torah scrolls (shields, finials, crowns, pointers in the shape of hands, etc.).
A category apart of these works of art consists in those related to the activities of the Burial Societies. The humane mission of these societies in the past centuries is recalled by alms boxes, ballot boxes for the elections of the presidium of the society, or various utensils (combs, cleaners). A unique artistic document affording a survey of the activities of the Prague Burial Society consists in a series of pictures painted by an anonymous artist about 1780.

The Maisel Synagogue and its artistic collections suggest a transition from the Renaissance and Baroque monuments of the Prague ghetto to modern times. From the end of the 17th century the ghetto was gradually becoming an overcrowded quarter with maximum density of houses. The poor living conditions were made worse by increasing taxes which affected the Jews much more heavily than their Christian neighbours. However, even under these circumstances the number of its inhabitants continued to grow, so that in the first third of the 18th century the Jewish population of Prague numbered 10—11 thousands. In the spirit of a certain "official antisemitism" the then authorities tried to reduce the Jewish population by the limitation of the number of Jewish families. In the reign of Maria Theresa, these attempts resulted even in a short-term expulsion of the Jews from Prague (1744—1748). The succession of Joseph II began to open gradually new possibilities to the Jews of Prague; for instance, the number of crafts and professions to which the Jews could apply their skills and which had been unknown to the mediaeval ghetto was growing.

In the spiritual field the tradition of rabbinic studies continued in the Prague ghetto also in the 18th and the 19th centuries. From the number of the scholars mention should be made of the Chief Rabbi and bibliophile, David Oppenheim (1664—1736), and his successors, Ezekiel Landau (1713—1793) and Eleazar Fleckeles (1754—1826).

The Decree of Tolerance of Joseph II of 1782 opened the way to religious understanding and gradual acquisition of equal rights by the Jews with their fellow citizens. Hand in hand with the following political and social reforms also the Jewish enlightenment ("Haskala") developed in accordance with European Enlightenment models. This movement endeavoured to eliminate the old anachronisms and prejudices dating from the Middle Ages, liken the Jewish population to its environment and achieve the modernization of its culture and the way of life. The devout learned rabbis were replaced in a relatively short period by a younger generation of scholars who combined their traditional faith with the research in the field of the new, speedily developing "Wissenschaft des Judentums" (Jewish Science). The number of the principal representatives of this stream in Prague included S.J. Rapoport (1790—1867), Leopold Zunz (1794—1886), Michael Sachs (1808—1864) or S.I. Kaempf (1818—1892).

Under the influence of the Enligtenment also reformed Jewish communities began originating in the first half of the 19th century, which created also a new type of synagogue service. The first reformed Jewish community in Prague was founded in the thirties of the 19th century around the Old Shul ("Altschul"). It was one of the oldest Prague synagogues which had been frequently damaged, destroyed and rebuilt in the course of centuries. Finally it was demolished and in 1868 the present-day Spanish Synagogue was built on its site with an interior richly decorated in Moorish style. In the reform community of the Old Shul František Škroup, the composer of the Czech national anthem "Where is my home?", worked as organist and choir-leader for several years.

In the period of 1848—1867, which brought about complete emancipation of the Jews in Bohemia and Moravia, the Prague ghetto was abolished as a secluded urban quarter, the Jews could live outside its walls and became full citizens in all respects. Therefore, new synagogues originated outside the former ghetto. The most important of them was the Jubilee Synagogue in the New Town of Prague, built in 1905—1906 in the spirit of the Art Nouveau (Jugendstil) and decorated in the much favoured pseudo-moorish style.

The break of the 19th and the 20th centuries, i.e. the last period of the existence of the old Prague ghetto (then a quarter of the poor), was simultaneously the period in which the Prague Jewish culture enriched significantly the world literature. It was the period of Franz Kafka (1883—1924), one of the greatest literary geniuses of the 20th century, who spent a major part of his life in Prague and its magic environment inspired him to his work. After his death in the Kierling sanatorium near Klosterneuburg his remains were brought to Prague and buried in the New Jewish Cemetery at Olšany, where a number of other representatives of Prague Jewry is buried.

Franz Kafka died in the Czechoslovak Republic, which originated on October 28, 1918. Under the leadership of its first president, T.G. Masaryk, and his successor E. Beneš, Czechoslovakia became an island of democracy in Central Europe of the period between the two world wars, in which the Jews enjoyed all civic rights and freedoms. A tragic break of the favourable development came with the Nazi occupation of Bohemia and Moravia and the Second World War. The Nazis introduced the ill-famed Nuremberg Laws to the territory of the so-called Protectorate of Bohemia and Moravia and began with a systematic persecution of the Jews culminating in their mass murders. In the North Bohemian fort city of Terezín (Theresienstadt) the Nazis established a concentration camp-ghetto to which the Jews from Bohemia, Moravia and some other countries were deported. In the period of the Holocaust some 80 000 Jews from Bohemia and Moravia perished and 153 Jewish communities were annihilated.

In the course of those few years also one of the phases of the history of the Prague Jewish Museum, which had been founded in 1906, took place. At the Nazi order the Jewish Museum became the place of concentration of the works of art from the property of abolished synagogues and Jewish communities. Among the memorials which originated directly in the Holocaust and enriched the collections of the renewed Jewish Museum after the war the deeply moving collection of several thousands of children's drawings is outstanding, which originated in the concentration camp-ghetto in Terezín. With a few exceptions their little authors died in the gas chambers of the Auschwitz concentration camp.

Although the Nazis murdered some six millions of Jews from all European countries in the course of the Second World War, they did not succeed to implement their intention to destroy all Jews incl. their religion and culture. Thus a Jewish community lives again in Prague, small in numbers, but strong in its resolution to maintain the millennial tradition of Prague Jewry. At present two synagogues are active in Prague — the Old New Synagogue and the Jubilee Synagogue. Prague is also the seat of the Council of Jewish Communities in the Czech Republic, the Prague Jewish community and the Rabbinate.

The millennial history of Prague Jewry was not closed, but continues. The depth and humanism of Jewish culture, existing in our country since the Middle Ages, is testified to inter alia by the collections of the Jewish Museum housed in the historical buildings of the former Prague ghetto.

Jan Minařík: The Old Jewish Cemetery (1899)
The romantic atmosphere of the cemetery with
tombstone groups amidst the islands of verdure
has been inspiring the artists from the
19th century to the present day

Overall view of the Old Jewish Cemetery, the chief burial ground of Prague Ghetto, in which some 12 000 tombstones have been preserved to our day

Typical tombstone groups, which originated in the course of four centuries by the gradual increase of the cemetery elevation by ever new layers of graves

The Nephele mound,
in which infants who had died during or immediately after their birth were buried. In 1903 the remains of the dead, buried in other parts of the cemetery, were brought here after the reduction of the cemetery area during the clearance of the ghetto

The fragments of Gothic tombstones from the 15th century,
found in the Vladislav Street in the New Town of Prague, where the remainders of an older Jewish cemetery were discovered in the middle of the 19th century

/ 30 / 31 /

Plain stelae from the 15th and the 16th centuries bear no decorations, but their Hebrew inscriptions carved in stone give a monumental impression

Facsimile of the tombstone of Avigdor Kara (1439) in the Old Jewish Cemetery
Avigdor Kara, poet and scholar, is the author of the elegy commemorating the pogrom of 1389, which took place in the ghetto of Prague

Levite laver
The picture of the laver, serving the ceremonial washing of the hands of the priests — cohens, can be found on the tombstones of the deceased who originated from the biblical tribe Levi according to tradition

The shield-bearing lions
decorate the tombstone of Hendl Bashevi (1628), wife of Jacob Bashevi, the first Jew in Bohemia to be raised to peerage with the title "of Treuenburg"

Symbol of traditional membership of a family of cohens
— two hands raised in benediction, marks the graves of the deceased who originated from the family of the first high priest, Aaron, according to tradition

The name of Jehuda-Löw is often symbolized by the Bohemian lion
— a typical figure on the tombstones of the Old Jewish Cemetery

The symbol of the name Dov or Baer
This frequent Jewish name is symbolized by a relief or a carving of a bear

A book symbolized the profession of Cantor, who leads the service in the synagogue

Gryphon belongs to the fantastic motifs found on the tombstones in the Old Jewish Cemetery, which have no bearing on the

The original tombstone of Avigdor Kara in the museum in the Klausen Synagogue
The text of the inscription dating from 1439 is heavily damaged. However, the name of the deceased is still legible in its upper part

Typical tombstone groups
The dense rows of tombstones contribute to the peculiar atmosphere of the Old Jewish Cemetery
>

ברוך אתה יי אלהינו מלך העולם
שהחיינו וקיימנו והגיענו לזמן הזה ׃

צורת הציד הקונן על מזה׳ כי לא יחרוך רמיה צידו׳ :
על כן שער ראשו מרט׳ והוא הנלוה יורץ ימרט׳

כשבא ראש השנה בליל מוצאי שבת מתחיל ואומר זה׳

ברוך אתה יי אלהינו מלך
העולם בורא פרי הגפן ׃
ברוך אתה יי אלהינו מלך
העולם אשר בחר בנו מכל
עם ורוממנו מכל לשון וקדשנו ׃

Illustration of the Book of Benedictions, Prague, 1514
The Hebrew "Book of Songs and Benedictions" is the second print which had left the press of the Prague printing house of the Gersonide family, founded by Gerson ben Shelomo Cohen

Illustration of the Prague Haggadah (1526)
The Haggadah, printed in the Gersonide printing shop and containing the text pertaining to the Pesah — Easter — ranks among famous Prague Hebrew publications

Inscription about the construction of the Pinkas Synagogue,
situated in its vestibule: "A man was born from the tribe of Levi, Aaron Meshullam by name . . . and he built this synagogue, a wonderful building, with his wife, daughter of Rabbi Menahem, mistress Nehama . . . In 1535 the work began and terminated to the honour of the Lord and the Torah here in the holy community, the royal Prague."

The Ark of the Pinkas Synagogue
has Late-Renaissance decorations. In front of it, in the centre of the synagogue, there is the lectern surrounded by an iron grille

Illustration of the Prague Haggadah (1526)
The Haggadah, printed in the Gersonide printing shop and containing the text pertaining to the Pesah — Easter — ranks among famous Prague Hebrew publications

סכום פסוקים דספרא וספרא דאורייתא ׃ בראשית אלף וחמש מאות
ושלשים וארבעה ׃ ואלה שמות אלף ומאתים ותשעה ׃ ויקרא שמנה
מאות וחמשים ותשעה ׃ במדבר סיני אלף ומאתים ושמונים ושמנה ׃
אלה הדברים אלף וחמשים וחמשה ׃ סכום הפסוקים של כל התורה
חמשת אלפים ותשע מאות וארבעים
וחמשה ׃

ברוך הנותן

ליעף כח

ולאין אונים

עצמה ירבה

גרשם בר שלמה הכהן מחקק ׃
מרדכי בר גרשם הכהן מחקק ׃
שלמה בר גרשם הכהן מחקק ׃

של זה החומש נאום אולעקש שאלטש בן יורג שולטש

The coat-of-arms of Prague in the Pentateuch of 1530
is framed by the verses from Isaiah (40, 29):
"Blessed He who giveth power to the faint, and to them who have no might he increaseth strength."

אלה

הדברים אשר דבר משה
אל כל ישראל בעבר הירדן
במדבר בערבה מול סוף בין
פארן ובין תפל ולבן וחצרת
ודי זהב׃ אחד עשר יום
מחרב דרך הר שעיר עד
קדש ברנע׃ ויהי בארבעים
שנה בעשתי עשר חדש

נחקק פה ק״ק פראגו
הבירה על ידי האחים בני
גרשם הכהן ונחקק שלמה
ומרדכי הכהן׳ שלמה
הכהן

The Prague Pentateuch of 1530
In this rare print particularly the richly decorated
title pages of the individual books of the

Inscription about the construction of the Pinkas Synagogue,
situated in its vestibule: "A man was born from the tribe of Levi, Aaron Meshullam by name . . . and he built this synagogue, a wonderful building, with his wife, daughter of Rabbi Menahem, mistress Nehama . . . In 1535 the work began and terminated to the honour of the Lord and the Torah here in the holy community, the royal Prague."

The Ark of the Pinkas Synagogue
has Late-Renaissance decorations. In front of it, in the centre of the synagogue, there is the lectern surrounded by an iron grille

Detail of the inner door to the Pinkas Synagogue
The door is decorated with a laver symbolizing the membership of the Horowitz family in the tribe of Levi

The vault of the Pinkas Synagogue shows the blending of the Late Gothic architecture with Renaissance elements

גור אריה יהודה

ביאור

שחבר הגאון האלוף נ״י כמוהר״ר יהודה בר בצלאל על פי׳ רש״י ז״ל על חמשה חומשי תורה

לבאר פירשו לתלמידים המעיינים כי ראשון הוא פירושו לכל פי׳ לפרש הפשט גם כ״ל מתלמוד ואגדת מדרש רבות מכלתא ספרא וספרי גם לברר דבריו אם האמת אתו מה שהשיבו עליו הבאים אחריו ולברר כל מה שבא בדבריו מדברי רז״ל אם בהלכה לברר עומק ההלכה ואם באגדה לבאר אותה על פי סודה וט״ב טעמה וזמן המאמרים הידועים שבאו בפי׳ רש״י ראיה על האחרים שכלם דברי חכמה וטוס א״ז בהם ובקצת מקומות להראות פי׳ במקרא או בתרגום יותר קרוב עד שהחבור הזה הוא נאות אף לגדול וה״א אריה בתורה ולינוק והכים נור כותר׳ לכן שם חבור הזה **גור אריה** והוא טרף יטרף כל פירוש זר ורחוק יביא עד הטרפה לא ישלם אורו כסף וזהב וכל חפצי לא ישוו בו כמו שאמר טוב לי

תורת פיך מאלפי
זהב וכסף

נדפס תחת ממשלת אדננו המיוחס הקיסר והמלך רומי רודולף יר״ה ותנשא מלכותו כ״י״א והוקם המלוכה ע״י ובבית הקצין הישיש היקר כמו״ר מרדכי ב״ר גרשם כ״ץ נ״ב מחוקק

פה ק״ק פראג הבירה בשנת של״ח לפ״ק

Title page of Rabbi Löw's book of 1578
The majority of the first editions of the works of Rabbi Löw was published in Prague by the Hebrew printing house of the Gersonide family

The tombstone of Rabbi Löw (1609) and his wife Perl (1610)
forms the spiritual centre of the Old Jewish Cemetery and the target of innumerable visitors who come here to say their prayers, drop their wishes into the tomb, or at least see the grave of the greatest thinker of the Prague ghetto

The tombstone of David Gans (1613) is decorated by the symbols of his name — David's star and the goose

The statue of Rabbi Löw by Ladislav Šaloun dates from 1911. It is installed near the new Prague townhall and recalls the legend on the struggle of Rabbi Löw with the Angel of Death

The tombstone of Joseph Solomon Delmedigo (1655)
This scientist, doctor and philosopher ranked among the foremost Jewish scholars of the 17th century. He spent the last years of his life in Prague

The tombstone of Jehuda Löw Teller (1697), the Jewish doctor in Prague, is decorated with the symbols of his name and profession — relief of a lion holding a doctor's lancet in his paw

The Ark of the High Synagogue
The High Synagogue was founded by Mordecai Maisel in 1568. The Baroque Ark is of a later date

Detail of the Ark of the High Synagogue shows an effective combinations of colours and the gilded Hebrew inscription

The curtain from the Old-New Synagogue, 1738
Synagogal textiles dazzle the visitors with their colour schemes, ornaments and the noble beauty of the Hebrew script

Detail of the curtain of 1738
The curtain was donated to the Old-New Synagogue by mistress Shifra, daughter of Wolf Spira and widow of the Chief Rabbi of Prague, David Oppenheim

A curtain, Prague, 1772
Synagogal curtains are suspended in front of the Ark protecting the parchment Torah scrolls with the Hebrew text of the Pentateuch

A curtain of folk type, Boskovice, 1831
The simplicity of expression dominates the textiles which originated in minor Jewish communities of Bohemia and Moravia, often under the influence of local folk art

Torah mantle, Březnice, 1761
Another basic type of synagogal textiles are Torah mantles, used for the wrapping of the parchment Torah scrolls

Detail of a Torah mantle, Prague, 1731
The mantle is decorated with rich embroidery on fine velvet. It was donated to the Pinkas Synagogue by Josef Weli and his wife

The motif of the Decalogue on a drapery has formed a frequent motif of recent synagogal art

Bags for the tefillin (phylacteries), Bohemia, 19th century,
are an example of minor Jewish textiles — products of non-professional household embroidery

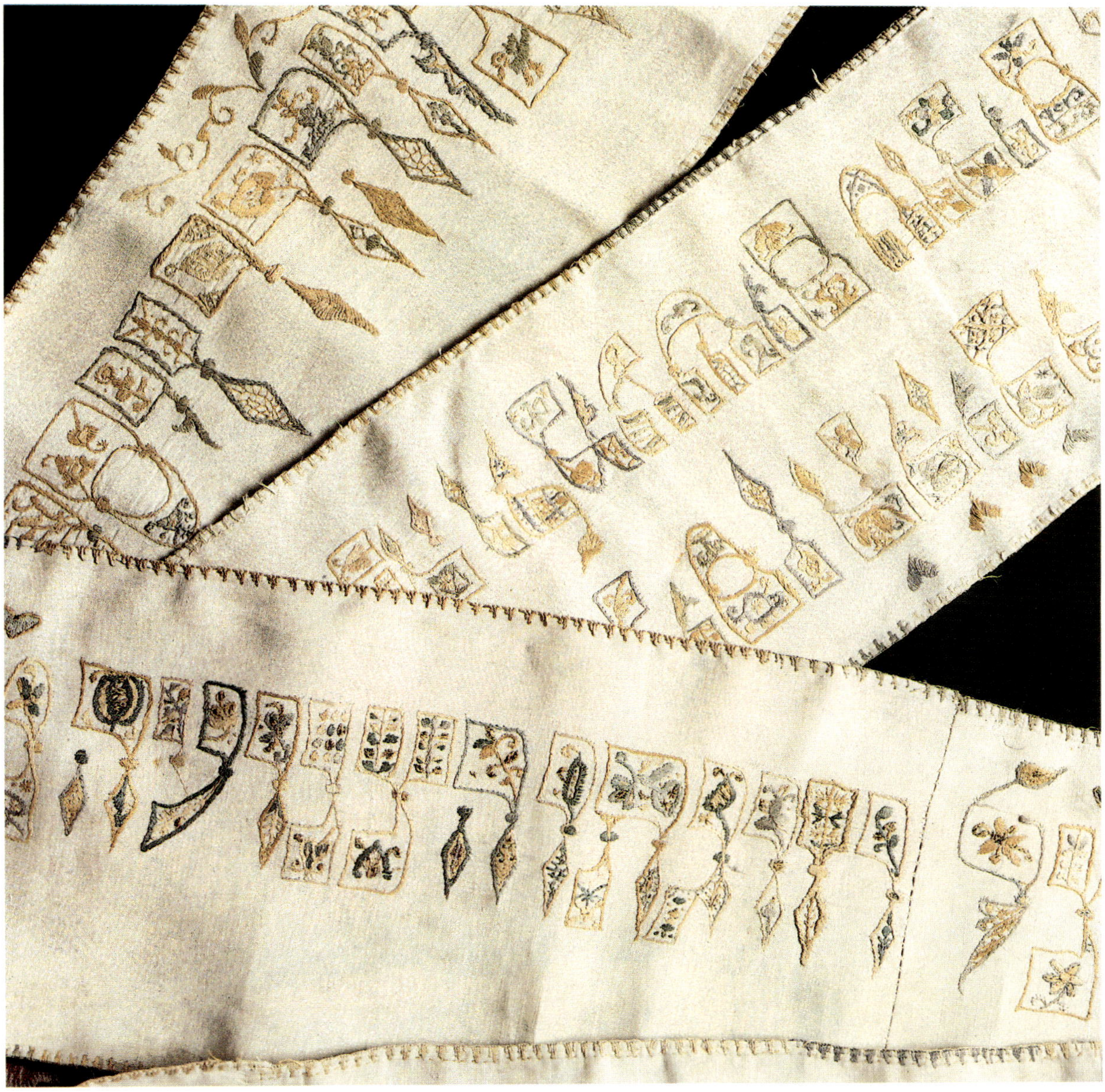

Torah binder, Mladá Boleslav, 1752
The binders are used to bind the parchment Torah scrolls. The custom of their embroidery on the occasion of the birth of a boy was widespread not only among Bohemian and Moravian Jews. The decoration comprises a Hebrew text wishing the boy healthy growth to the study of the Torah, marriage and good deeds

Skullcaps, Bohemia, the 19th century
Richly embroidered skullcaps are intended for the head of the family to wear on holidays

David's star with a hat — the emblem of the Jewish community of Prague
It can be found on the façade and on the top of the turret of the Jewish Townhall, on the banner of the Jewish community of Prague in the Old-New Synagogue and on more recent tombstones of the Old Jewish Cemetery

Two clocks marking the same time
or — in the words of Guillaume Apollinaire:
"Les aiguilles de l'horloge du quartier juif vont
à rebours /Et tu recules aussi dans ta vie
lentement/ En montant au Hradchin . . ."

/ 66 / 67 /

The Ark of the Maisel Synagogue
Mordecai Maisel " . . . erected also a great synagogue, so magnificent that it has no equal in beauty in the whole Diaspora; he erected it on twenty pillars, all of which are of hewn stone . . . And it is counted that the construction cost him . . . more than ten thousand thalers . . ."

Tympanum of the entrance door to the Maisel Synagogue
The original Renaissance building was damaged by the fire of 1689 and was rebuilt several times later on

The vault of the Maisel Synagogue
The last reconstruction at the break of the 19th and the 20th centuries implanted false ribs in the synagogue vault

Window in the Maisel Synagogue
Its stained glass vitrailles formed part of the Neo-Gothic reconstruction

יהוה

Torah shield, 1770
Silver shields are suspended on the Torah wrapped in the mantle. They are often decorated with the figures of Moses and Aaron and the columns which stood at the entrance to the Temple of Solomon in Jerusalem

Animal motifs on a brass Hanukkah lamp
(about 1800)
The lamps of this type are used on the Hanukkah, celebrated in commemoration of the liberation and re-consecration of the Temple of Jerusalem during the Maccabee uprising in the 2nd cent. B.C.

Pointers, Bohemia and Moravia, the 19th century
They are used to follow the text of the Torah during its reading to prevent human hand from touching the parchment

Spice box, Prague, 1840
Silver, often richly decorated spice boxes are used at the ceremony of leavetaking of the Sabbath

Pewter seder plate, 1775
Seder plates belong to a festively decorated table on the eve of the Pesah — the Jewish Easter

Goblet, 1745
In the collection of synagogal silver the festive goblets are frequent, often decorated with Hebrew dedication inscriptions

Citrus fruit bowl, Prague, 1860
The citrus fruit — ethrog — is one of the plant symbols used in the holiday of Sukkoth (the Feast of Tabernacles) which is of agricultural character

Silver Hanukkah lamp, the 19th century

Levite laver and basin, the 18th century
The symbols of the laver or of the whole set can be found on tombstones and on synagogal objects as the sign of the tribe of Levi

Sabbath candlestick, the 19th century
These candlesticks are used for candles illuminating the festive table on the Sabbath — the day of rest and peace

Torah crown, Brno, 1813
The silver crowns decorate the Torah scrolls at
the time of big holidays

Interior of the Klausen Synagogue in the middle of the 19th century
The synagogue, founded by Mordecai Maisel, was named after several minor buildings — the Klausen — on the site of which it was erected

The Klausen Synagogue
In its present form it was built after the great fire of the Prague ghetto in 1689 which devastated the original building erected by Mordecai Maisel, the mayor of the Jewish Town

Detail of the Ark
The Baroque Ark is richly decorated and covered with gilded Hebrew inscriptions

The Ark of the Klausen Synagogue dates from 1696. Its donator was Samuel Oppenheim

Stucco vault decoration of the Klausen Synagogue
After the Old-New Synagogue the Klausen Synagogue was the second most important synagogue of the Prague ghetto and the reserved prayer house of the Prague Burial Society

Window of the Klausen Synagogue
The windows of the synagogue received their stained glass vitrailles during the partial reconstruction of the synagogue in the eighties of the 19th century

Ceremonial hall of the Burial Society, a pseudo-Romanesque building from the beginning of the 20th century. At present it houses the permanent exhibition of children's drawings from the concentration camp-ghetto of Terezín

Art Nouveau entrance grille and the stairs in the Ceremonial Hall

והוא רחום

From the cycle of paintings of the Prague Burial Society
The Burial Society originated in Prague as early as 1564. Around 1780 an unknown painter painted a cycle of pictures recording the activities of the Society; in the first half of the 19th century the cycle was supplemented with several additions
∧ >

An alms box (1780) and a comb for the hair of the deceased (1813)
were the property of the Burial Societies which had existed in a number of Jewish communities

Pitcher of the Burial Society, Miroslav, 1813
The pitchers were used during the annual meetings of the Burial Societies, combined with a festive dinner. They are decorated with the scenes from the society activities

Tombstone of David Oppenheim (1736)
The Chief Rabbi of Prague, David Oppenheim, buried in the Old Jewish Cemetery, amassed a huge collection of Hebrew prints and manuscripts, at present kept in the Bodleian Library in Oxford

"The Holy Society performing good deeds"
A gilt inscription above the entrance to the Ceremonial Hall interprets the Hebrew name of the Burial Society

חברא קדישא
גומלי חסדים

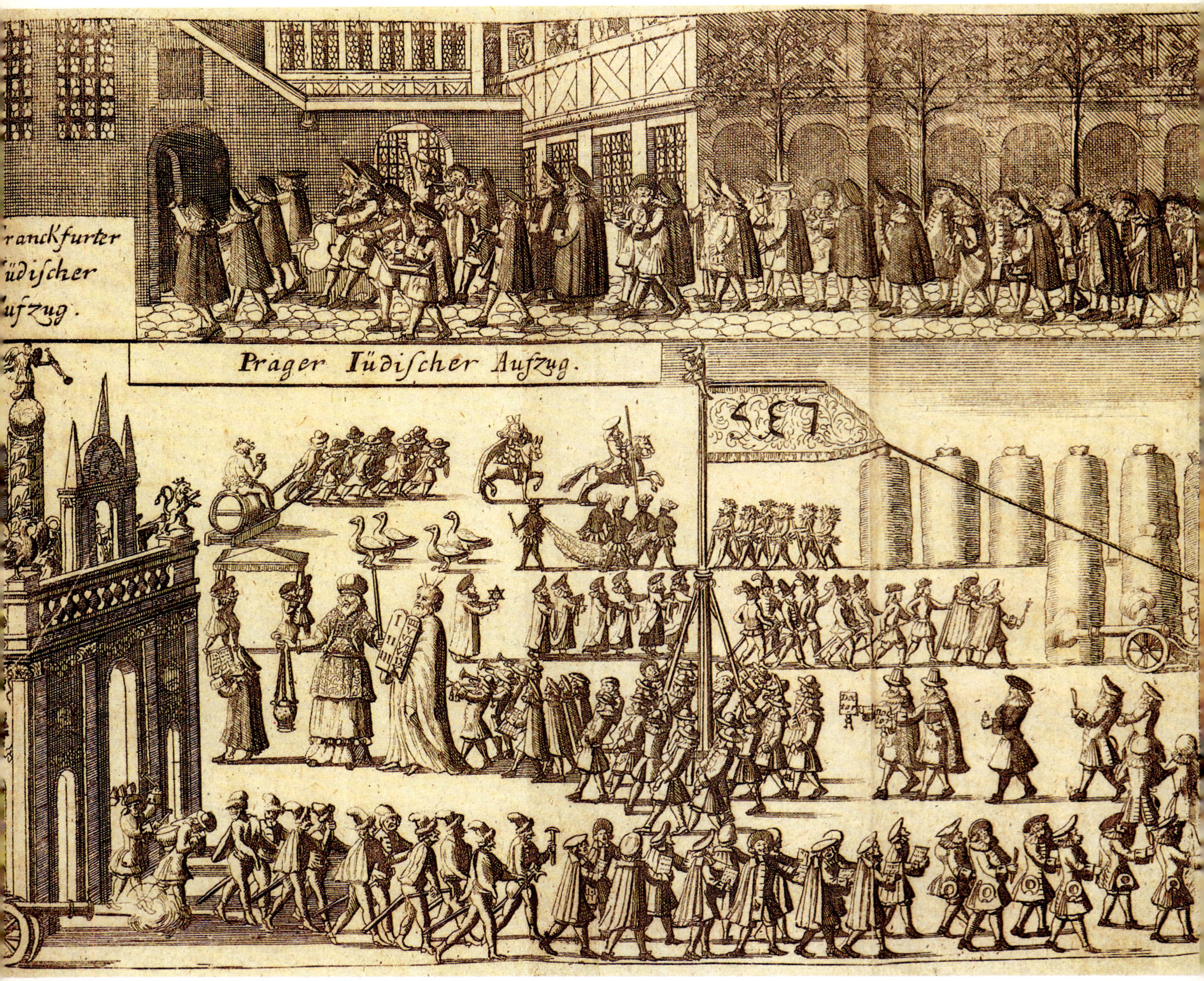

Festive procession of Prague Jews in 1716 took place during the celebrations of the birth of Prince Leopold, son of Emperor Charles VI. Both banners of the Prague Jewish community were carried in the procession

The cross on the Charles Bridge (1696)
The Hebrew inscription, supplementing the Baroque sculpture, is a quotation from Isaiah (6, 3): "Holy, holy, holy is the Lord of hosts"

קדוש
I·N·R·I

The portrait of Eleazar Fleckeles,
Chief Rabbi of Prague and representative of traditional rabbinic studies. The scholar is portrayed with his most widely known work, a collection of answers to religious and legal questions

The portrait of S. J. Rapoport,
Chief Rabbi of Prague and scholar, dates from
the forties of the 19th century and is ascribed to

The Old Shul in the middle of the 19th century
The appearance of the Old Shul, the many times rebuilt oldest Prague synagogue on the right-hand bank of the river Vltava, is known today only from old engravings

The Spanish Synagogue
Its western façade, with its arched windows and lace-like decorations bordering its roofs, recalls an Oriental castle

The vault of the Spanish Synagogue
The synagogue obtained its name from its decorations the coloured and gilded stucco of which imitates the arabesques of the Moorish style

The Ark of the Spanish Synagogue
The pseudo-Oriental architecture of the façade is
repeated also in the design of the Ark

Near the entrance to the Ark
of the Spanish Synagogue
The motif of the six-pointed star forms the principal element of the decoration of the whole interior, wall paintings and ballustrade carvings

The Jubilee Synagogue
The pseudo-Moorish style, so fashionable in European synagogues built at the break of the 19th and the 20th centuries, differentiates markedly the Jubilee Synagogue from the neighbouring buildings

The pseudo-Moorish elements in the decoration of the façade of the Jubilee Synagogue — several times repeated arches of the entrance doors, high and slender columns and multiple windows with ogee arches

The Art Nouveau grille in the front of the Jubilee Synagogue
The Art Nouveau and the Moorish elements supplement each other excellently

Women's gallery of the Jubilee Synagogue, the interior of which is painted by light penetrating through stained glass windows
>

Věnovali Moric a Růžena Bäckovi
Věnovali Albin a Růžena Ho
שלום בחילך

Věnovali
Marta a Arnošt Fischmannovi

Interior of the Jubilee Synagogue
The long and high principal nave is illuminated by historical chandeliers suspended from the ceiling decorated with floral motifs

Ceremonial Hall of the New Jewish Cemetery, serving its purpose to the present day. It was built in the Neo-Renaissance style at the end of the 19th century

The tombstone of S. I. Kaempf (1892)
The Neo-Renaissance sarcophagus covers the remains of one of the most important Central European representatives of modern Hebrew and Jewish studies who acted also as preacher in the Spanish Synagogue

The vault of the family Bondy,
Prague enterpreneurs and patrons of arts and sciences. One of its members, the follower of the Czecho-Jewish movement, Bohumil Bondy, participated in the edition of historical sources to the history of the Jews in Bohemia and Moravia

FRANZ KAFKA
HERMANN KAFKA
JULIE KAFKA

The grave of Franz Kafka,
the most frequently visited spot of the New Jewish Cemetery

Memorial tablet on the site of Franz Kafka's native house
on the former "Three Well Square", where the Prague ghetto used to end once

Iron synagogue grille, the 18th century
The products of smith's art decorated the lecterns and railings of women's galleries in urban and rural synagogues

Silver binding of a prayer book, the 20th century
Such a prayer book was a luxury present for the wedding or an anniversary

Seder plate, Karlovy Vary, 1890,
an example of how even the plates intended for traditional dinner table featured fashionable genre scenes

Festive goblets of ruby glass, Bohemia,
the 19th century
Hebrew inscriptions indicate that the goblets were used on the Sabbath or on holidays

Decorative binding of a prayer book, the 18th century,
accentuating the contents of festive prayers

Shofar,
a ram's horn, the sound of which can be heard in the synagogues on the New Year (Rosh ha-Shana) and the Day of Atonement (Yom Kippur)

Carvings of the Ark from Podbořanský Rohozec, 1816

ווען מן זיכט בתי כנסיות דיא טין גיבויט זיין זוא
מאכט מן דיזא ברכה

בָּרוּךְ אַתָּה ה׳ אֱמֶ״הָ מַצִּיב גְּבוּל
אַלְמָנָה ❖

וויבר טוועקדיזי קרייטר מאכט מן דיא ברכה

בָּרוּךְ אתה ה׳ אֱלֹהֵינוּ מֶלֶךְ הָעוֹלָם
בּוֹרֵא עִשְׂבֵי בְשָׂמִים

A folk manuscript of prayers and benedictions,
Moravia, the 18th century,
belongs to minor charming works of Jewish
scribes — illuminators

Illustrated Scroll of Esther, the 18th century Biblical text read in synagogues on the Feast of Purim, is decorated with the drawings of figures and scenes from the story of Queen Esther

The wooden Ark of folk type,
Podbořanský Rohozec, 1816
The wooden Empire Ark, richly carved and polychromed, is an example of cabinet-making craft in rural settlements

The statue of Moses by František Bílek,
the work of a Czech artist of the 20th century, on
the background of one of the oldest monuments
of Gothic architecture in Prague

The Old Jewish Cemetery
>>>

The GHETTO of Prague

PHOTOS BY JIŘÍ MACHT

TEXT BY

VLADIMÍR SADEK AND JIŘINA ŠEDINOVÁ

Designed by Vladimír Sadek and Jiřina Šedinová
Translated by Slavoš Kadečka
Cover and graphic design by Antonín Kalcovský
Published by the Olympia Publishing House, Prague 1992, as its 2610th publication
1st edition, 126 pages, 125 colour photos
Responsible editor: Soňa Scheinpflugová
Art editor: Karel Kárász
Technical editor: Zbyněk Zajíček
Printed by Svoboda
27-005-92

die Altneusy